P9-ELI-277

BIRDING BASICS

BIRDING BASICS

Sandy Cortright

Sterling Publishing Co., Inc. New York

Edited by Jeanette Green
Designed by Jan Melchior
Photos by Sandy Cortright, except where otherwise credited

Library of Congress Cataloging-in-Publication Data

Cortright, Sandy.
    Birding basics / by Sandy Cortright.
        p.   cm.
    Includes index.
    ISBN 0-8069-1262-6
    1. Bird-watching. 2. Birds—Identification. [1. Bird-watching.
    2. Birds—Identification.] I. Title.
    QL677.5.C76   1995
    598'.07234—dc20   94-27655
                                                   CIP
                                                     AC

2 4 6 8 10 9 7 5 3 1

Published by Sterling Publishing Company, Inc.
387 Park Avenue South, New York, N.Y. 10016
© 1995 by Sandy Cortright
Distributed in Canada by Sterling Publishing
% Canadian Manda Group, One Atlantic Avenue, Suite 105
Toronto, Ontario, Canada M6K 3E7
Distributed in Great Britain and Europe by Cassell PLC
Wellington House, 125 Strand, London WC2R 0BB, England
Distributed in Australia by Capricorn Link (Australia) Pty Ltd.
P.O. Box 6651, Baulkham Hills, Business Centre,
NSW 2153, Australia
Printed and bound in Hong Kong
All rights reserved

Sterling ISBN 0-8069-1262-6

cover photo, savanna sparrow; back cover, American white pelicans; p. 1, tricolored
blackbird; p. 2, black-necked stilt; p. 6, robin chat, © JOHN DELEVORYAS

Acknowledgments

It is a great pleasure to acknowledge the help and encouragement I've received from many people for this book. They have my eternal gratitude for sharing their talents and resources.

Many thanks to:

- Mike Danzenbaker, John Delevoryas, Neal Enault, Charles H. Newman, John R. Silliman, Don Slaiter, and Ken Eugene from the Bay Area Bird Photographers for sharing their photos and technical advice

- Santa Clara Valley Audubon Society members for helping me learn the joy of birding

- Dan Lloyd for supplying computer graphics

- John Aikin, ornithologist at the San Francisco Zoological Gardens, for answering my endless curious questions

- Andrea Green for being my writing mentor

- My sons, Jason and Brad Cortright, for learning to live with a birder and who are becoming birders, too

- And especially to Charles H. Newman for editing my rough manuscript and being willing, rain or shine, to stalk elusive birds with me

Contents

Yellow-necked spur fowl

© JOHN DELEVORYAS

Why Birding and Who Does It?

Young and old, rich or poor, we all marvel at birds' beauty and ability to fly. Tributes to these wonderful creatures and the songs they sing fill our music and literature. Birds and bird feathers have appeared in numerous artworks and adorned the human figure. We've even attempted to imitate the way they fly. Easily the most recognizable form of animal life, birds can be seen just about everywhere—on rocks and mountains, in deserts and swamps, around lakes and oceans, and over icy straits and tropical canopies.

Today, bird-watching is an international pastime. Bird-watchers number in the millions. Many different kinds of people enjoy birding whether as casual backyard observers or as avid birders who trek through miles or kilometres of jungles or wilderness to see rare species. Not so amazingly, people spend billions on wild birdseed each year. With contemporary interest in ecology, bird-watchers monitor the relative health of the earth's environment in their study of avian populations. Preservation of bird and other animal species has become an international concern and the subject of much controversy. Growing public interest in nature conservation and animal preservation has boosted membership in nature societies at an astonishing rate worldwide.

Birding appeals to both children and adults. Besides getting people outdoors, this hobby costs very little to begin, and you can enjoy it life-long. Since birds are frequent visitors to our neighborhoods, we can see them with relative ease in all seasons.

In this book, we'll explore birding fundamentals from what you need to get started to key field marks that identify each bird species. By learning a few tricks from the pros, you'll soon be able to improve your observation skills. And, before you know it, you'll be able to identify common birds without a moment's hesitation.

© JOHN DELEVORYAS

Great blue heron

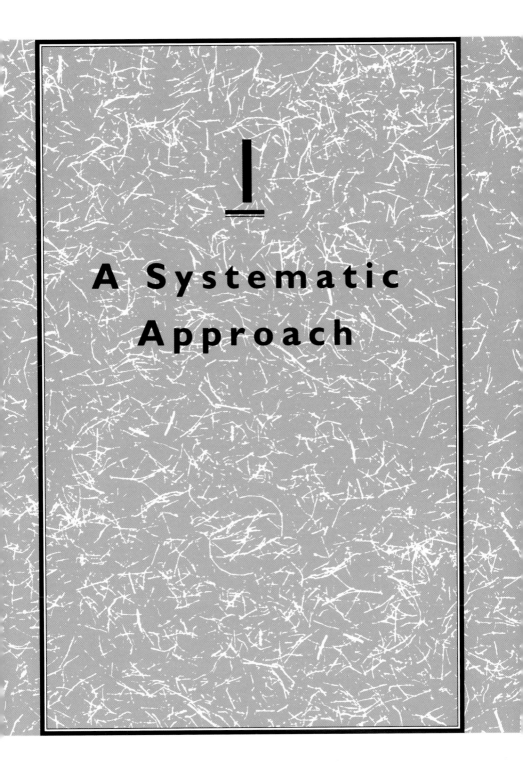

I

A Systematic Approach

B ird-watching is a pleasurable activity you can enjoy at many different levels. Many people just want to go outside and hike around to see birds, any birds. Then, others enjoy identifying *what* birds they see. And finally, there are dedicated birders who thrive on the challenge of finding and identifying as many species as possible. Casual hikers often have their curiosity piqued and may turn from passive observers to serious, hard-core birders.

Louis Pasteur said, "In the fields of observation, chance favors the mind that is prepared." While Pasteur, father of pasteurization, may not have

Migrating ducks take time to rest.

been a bird-watcher, what he said certainly holds true in birding as it does in science and many other activities. With a systematic approach and a little homework before going into the field, you can reap many benefits as well as great pleasure.

Birders use what we could call the process of elimination when identifying a species. Since there are nearly 8,600 species of bird worldwide, it would take forever to thumb through a field guide to identify an individual bird. But doing a little homework and being aware of what you'll probably see in the field, you'll be able to narrow possibilities to just a few choices.

Create Your Own Bird Sanctuary

For many birders, the best place to watch is from an easy chair in front of a window. Since it provides the basic needs of food, water, and shelter, birds will find your garden hospitable.

Start by offering water in a birdbath. When they discover this source of drinking water and bathing spa, you'll find plenty of action. A simple shallow pie pan of water or a potted plant saucer is a simple and adequate source. Of course, birdbaths on pedestals look nice too. A bubbling fountain will increase the visitors to your garden considerably because of its sound. No matter what kind of birdbath you choose, remember to clean it thoroughly every few days and replenish the water supply.

Bird feeders are a great way to coax birds to go where you can get a clear view of them. First, decide which type of bird you want to attract. A large, flat board with a moulding to form a raised edge will attract ground-feeding birds. Hummingbirds need a special feeder that contains nectar and that can be hung from a tree branch or the eaves of a roof. Hanging seed feeders are also popular.

A house finch and a chestnut-backed chickadee enjoy a hanging birdbath.

Decide which kind of birdseed each type of bird you want to attract will eat. Not all birds will come to a feeder. Insect-eaters take care of themselves and ignore even the choicest seeds. A wild bird or feed store may provide information on the

The Anna's hummingbird is the only hummingbird to winter in the western United States.

The male house finch varies from dark red to almost yellow coloring.

type of seed each species likes. Bread crumbs are not very nutritious, and they can actually harm a bird by not providing it the needed energy to survive. Grocery store birdseed tends to be heavy on milo, the seed birds least like but that's cheap to buy. If you want to attract lots of birds, give them a hearty meal of sunflower seeds, red or white millet, thistle (niger), cracked corn, or oat groats. You can purchase these seeds in mixes or by bulk.

Suet feeders attract many birds such as nuthatches, chickadees, and woodpeckers. Look for commercial blocks of suet at a bird supply store.

Slice an orange or apple and see if a visitor eats them. This is a real treat for fruit-eating species. Raw peanuts are good too!

Placing feeders near windows is ideal for armchair birders. Be sure there's a branch or plant nearby to ensure a safety zone of escape for shy birds. Locate feeders away from where people walk, since birds leave droppings. Also, locate feeders 8 feet (2.5 m) away from where squirrels can jump to them. Often a metal pole-mounted feeder is best, with a saucer-like squirrel guard placed to discourage any climbing creatures. A hardware or garden store will have these in stock, but squirrels are resourceful acrobats.

For shelter, bushes, trees, and brush piles are desirable. Birdhouses attract a few species, but not all birds take advantage of them.

When landscaping your garden, opt for the native species of plants since they'll be hearty and insect- or disease-resistant. If you forego the more delicate plant varieties, you won't have to use insecticides. Insects living in your garden can be a fine food source for birds.

A backyard feeding station will attract many species of bird.

Four Keys to Success

After you locate a bird, you need to eliminate *improbable* species so that you can quickly decide on *probable* possibilities. Consider these four things.

1. Where did you find the bird? Eliminate all birds not known in that habitat, geographic location, and elevation. See chapter 2 for comments about field guides that may provide this information.

2. Time of year determines movement in some bird populations. Chances are pretty good that you won't find a hummingbird in snowy mountains in December. Knowing when and where the bird migrates will help eliminate it from your list of possibilities. See chapter 3 for more information on migration.

3. Look at the general physical traits of the bird—size (bigger than a thrush?), body shape (plump or streamlined?), shape of bill (hooked or probing?), legs (long or short?). Also observe the bird's behavior. (Is it seen in flocks or individually? Does it have a notable flight pattern? How does it feed?) See chapter 4 for more detailed information.

4. Characteristics and field marks of the bird species will help narrow choices for your final identification. See identifying field marks in chapter 4.

By learning basic bird families and a few common examples in each group, you'll be well on your way to speedy identification. Consult chapter 5 for descriptions and photos of several common birds a birder might see that are found throughout the world. Knowing a little about each bird family, you'll soon establish a basic foundation of knowledge from which you'll be able to make comparisons.

The cactus wren builds a nest in desert cactus.

The woodpecker makes a nest in a tree trunk.

© JOHN DELEVORYAS

Lilac-breasted roller

2

Getting Started

Bird-watching is fun and, with practice, easy to do. Whether you're out in the countryside or in your own backyard, all you have to do is look around to see birds. With a good pair of binoculars and a field guide, you're all set for this wonderful pastime.

Experienced birders on safari.

Picking Out the Right Binoculars

Using a good pair of binoculars means the difference between having a good day and a *great* day of birding. Being able to obtain a close-up view increases your chances of identifying the bird and enhances your experience of bird-watching.

Binoculars come in many different sizes. Look for something that suits your needs as well as your budget. Consider these factors when making your selection—magnification, field, illumination, weight, and size.

Good beginning binoculars, for example, would be, say, 7 × 35. The first number indicates the *magnification* and the second, the *field*. You'll find these numbers written near the binoculars' eyepieces. So, for 7 × 35 binoculars, the 7 tells you that the object viewed through the small end of the glasses is magnified seven times. The 35 indicates the size or diameter in millimetres (here, 35 mm) of the large lens at the binoculars' opposite end. The larger the number of this (large) lens, the more light it receives. That also means that the viewer will be able to see a larger field or area through the glasses. This makes it easier to locate a moving bird.

The binoculars' *illumination*, or light transmission, is the amount of light that comes through the large-lens end of the binoculars. Coated lenses reduce glare and transmit more light than uncoated lenses.

A general rule when shopping for binoculars is to choose those with a 1-to-5 ratio, for example, 7 × 35 or 8 × 40. This ratio is ideal for use in low light and when it's hard to distinguish colors.

Consider the binoculars' *weight* and *size*. The 8 × 40 binoculars will show more detail, but they'll also be heavier. After a while, these might become uncomfortable. It's also more difficult to keep large, heavy glasses steady. On the other hand, small, lightweight glasses are great for tucking into a pocket, but they lose their capability for gathering light in low-light conditions. So, that would limit early morning and evening bird-watching.

Large 10 × 50 binoculars may require a tripod to hold them steady. These binoculars are usually preferred by advanced birders.

Binoculars should have caps around the eyepieces to aid people wearing glasses. Most binoculars come with these rubber or plastic caps, called an eye-relief feature.

Center-focusing binoculars are easy to adjust and most practical for bird-watching. Talk to a reputable dealer about what kind might be best for you. A dealer can advise you and demonstrate a variety of models.

Remember, even though . bird-watching is a relatively inexpensive pastime, it's important to have good binoculars. Buying poor quality or bargain-basement binoculars will limit your viewing pleasure. Try out several kinds before choosing yours. And, above all, don't buy them until you've tried viewing outdoors. Talk

with fellow bird-watchers, naturalists, and outdoors people. Ask what kind of binoculars they use and why they like or dislike them. Since you're making an investment, it's important to do your homework. This little bit of work will pay off in years of pleasure.

Use them to scan the sky, trees, and terrain for birds or to verify what you've seen with the naked eye.

How to Focus Binoculars Setting center-focusing binoculars is simple. Just follow these five steps to adjust the eyepieces for viewing closer than 80 feet (24 metres).

In the high trees are roosting American crows.

1. Select a target object about 300 feet (90 metres) away, and focus on this.

2. With both eyes, look through the binoculars, and bend the hinge at the center until you see only one circular image.

3. Using the center-focusing wheel for adjustment, close your right eye and look through the left eyepiece. Rotate the focusing wheel until you obtain a sharp image.

4. Close your left eye, and adjust the right eyepiece until the image is sharp. Once set, you don't need to readjust this eyepiece.

5. Look using both eyes. Is the target object in sharp focus? If not, repeat steps 2 to 4.

Now that you've adjusted your binoculars, practise using them. From now on, the only adjustment you'll need will be with the center-focus.

Using Binoculars Locate a target object with the naked eye and focus on it. Don't take your eyes off the object. Lift the binoculars to your eyes with both hands, and adjust the center focusing wheel with your middle finger. This takes a little practice, but it will pay off when you're trying to follow a moving bird. Sometimes it's easier to focus on a nearby stationary object, such as a branch, near the target.

Don't get frustrated. With practice you'll improve until focusing becomes second nature. Remember, the key to success is practice. Try to locate a large stationary object, such as a tree, when starting out. After you've mastered that, try a slow-moving object, like a distant airplane. Then, locate something faster, like a moving car, and finally, birds.

First try a large bird like an Australian pelican, found perhaps in an aviary.

Spotting Scopes

For the serious birder proficient in identifying birds, a spotting scope is an extra aid. Keep in mind that a spotting scope isn't a substitute for binoculars. Together, the two complement each other.

As with binoculars, the first number indicates magnification (small lens), and the second number (for the objective lens or large end) indicates how many millimetres of light-gathering surface the scope has.

As with binoculars, there's a trade-off in what you can see with different magnifications. In fixed-power spotting scopes, the most popular magnifications are $20 \times$ and $25 \times$. As the magnification increases, the field of view and light decreases. Usually $30 \times$ is about as high as a good scope can go before haze and mirages degrade the image quality.

Eyepieces can be straight or angled. The straight ones seem easier to use because where they point is what you see. The disadvantage of a straight spotting scope is the neck strain you might feel after using it for extended periods of time. Angled eyepieces have several different angles, with a 45-degree angle the most often used.

Eyepieces can be focused by either turning the eyepiece or rotating a separate knob or ring. Focusing a spotting scope usually takes longer than focusing with binoculars.

Some spotting scopes have interchangeable eyepieces that give a range of magnification from $15 \times$ to as much as $60 \times$. Wide-angle eyepieces are on the market as well. Zoom eyepieces are also available, which give a wide viewing field at lower magnification as one scans large open areas. When you spot birds, you can zoom the spotting scope to a higher magnification for a closer look. Some disadvantages of zooms include:

- *Cost—the eyepieces are much more costly than fixed lenses.*
- *A zoom usually has a slightly narrower field of view.*
- *The resolution isn't as sharp.*
- *The eye relief on zoom eyepieces is somewhat shorter than that of fixed-power eyepieces.*

The larger the objective lens, the brighter and higher resolution the image viewed. Either a 50 mm or 60 mm lens is a popular size. The smaller the lens, the less light gathered, and that limits shadowy or dusk and dawn use of the scope. If it were any larger, the weight would be prohibitive when you're out in the field. As with binoculars, think about the weight you'll be carrying. Remember, you need to mount the spotting scope on a tripod and that adds to your load.

Options for spotting scopes will raise the cost, but may be well worth the expense.

- *Waterproof scopes have hermetically sealed eyepieces which can't be easily interchanged. If you're in a damp, wet environment and could easily get splashed, this feature is worth considering.*
- *Rubber armor is for protection against bumps and abrasion, not to mention the occasional hard drop. Many birders claim that it's easier to hold, especially on cold days. This armor doesn't add waterproofing, but it will add weight.*
- *Protective coating will guard against scratches on the lenses.*

Tripods have varying features that only you can assess. Some scope owners prefer a video-camera tripod, while others prefer one suitable for cameras. Ask spotting-scope owners why they chose that particular style and if they're satisfied with their choice. Dealers usually carry many styles of spotting scopes and tripods. Just remember, it's a one-time purchase and you get what you pay for. The extra cost, when pro-rated over many years of use, is small indeed, compared to the pleasure a spotting scope gives. If expense is a factor, investigate good quality used equipment before buying new, inferior-quality goods.

Dressing for Birding

There is no official uniform or dress code for birding. Using practical sense is the best rule to follow. Consider the weather, location of your birding activities, and amount of time you plan to spend outdoors.

Shoes Starting with your best foot forward, pick shoes and boots that fit well and keep your feet warm and dry. Those with a heel are safer for preventing slips and falls and are preferable to the flat-sole style. Waterproofing is a must. For rugged terrain and long hikes, a high-top style might give your feet and ankles more support. It's also a good idea to take another pair of shoes along in case the unthinkable happens, and you end up with wet feet or worse. Sometimes rubber boots are preferable in wet, swampy areas, not to mention barnyards and muddy bogs. For warm weather and around more civilized environments, walking shoes are popular as well as the old standby, sneakers. Taking along an extra pair of lightweight shoes to change into after an all-day excursion wearing heavy boots is a good idea too.

Socks Wearing heavy socks will protect feet from blister as well as the cold. Some birders wear two pairs for early morning hikes and take off one pair as the temperature warms up. Check with a sporting goods store for special knit hiking socks that have extra cushioning on the heel and sole areas. Many brands of socks have a special yarn that wicks perspiration away from the body. Kneesocks can be worn with shorts to protect the legs.

Long Underwear This is an absolute must in cold weather. Whether you prefer one- or two-piece suits, or only a top or bottom, long underwear can save the day. Many types of materials are avail-

able and choosing the right weight depends on how cold the temperature is that you'll be experiencing. For mild to cold temperatures, silk long underwear is preferred. This versatile fabric is warm, not bulky, and it can be folded into a pocket or backpack when it's no longer needed. For the hearty birder who ventures out in freezing temperatures, there's a wide range of thermal fabrics made to warm even the coldest body. Most sporting goods stores carry long underwear in a wide range of sizes and colors.

Pants There's only one general rule: be comfortable. Birders wear every kind of pants imaginable. Long pant legs protect against scratches and insects and keep the legs from getting sunburned, too. For cold weather, a heavier fabric is practical. If you don't like the feeling of long underwear, flannel-lined pants are on the market. Warm-up pants are another alternative. Shorts, both long and short, are great for warm weather. Small items such as car keys, tissues, wallet, and lip balm fit easily into pockets.

Shirts Layers seem to be the most practical. Start with a cotton pullover and add a sweatshirt or sweater. Any more shirts will become too bulky and using long underwear might be your best bet. Long sleeves on a hot day might seem uncomfortable, but consider the protection from getting sunburn, poisonous plants, and biting insects sleeves afford you. Loose-fitting shirts are comfortable even on hot days.

Jackets Windbreakers are wonderful on a mild, breezy day. These lightweight jackets easily fold into a backpack or wrap around the waist or shoulders when it's warm. Styles featuring a zip-out lining can serve birders almost year-round. Jackets with hoods are great protection around the neck and eliminate the need for a hat. Fold-up collars protect the neck from sunburn, windburn, and cold breezes. Pockets are essential for hands, gloves, field guides, handkerchiefs, pencils, and notepads. Heavier weight lined jackets are needed for cold weather birding and provide comfort on the chilliest of days. Long jackets add warm protection for hips and thighs.

Vests Is it possible to have too many pockets? For every pocket, there seems to be something to put in it. Photographers' vests may have a dozen pockets, and travellers' vests have as many as eight places to stow items. Mesh fabric styles are terrific for warm weather birding or can be worn under a windbreaker. Lined quilted fabric vests can serve as a layer under a jacket in colder temperatures. Look for them in sporting goods, photography, or department stores, or check mail order catalog companies.

Hats Hats are the best body-heat regulators you can have. Since in winter, most of our body heat leaves through the top of the head, a sensible hat is standard equipment. Broad brims shade and protect from the harmful rays of the sun and if there's a breeze, a chin strap, elastic band, or some type of tie will keep your headgear from flying off with the birds. Straw and lightweight fabric hats are popular on sunny, warm days, while wool, acrylic, and felt hats can be worn in cold weather. Knit stocking caps, baseball caps, and visors are but a few of the many kinds of hats birders wear.

Gloves On those chilly days, gloves feel wonderful. Unlined stretchable nylon fabric allows you to use your fingers to adjust binoculars and write notes. Some birders like the warm knit gloves with finger tips cut off. This frees the finger tips for fine tuning the binoculars and turning the pages of the field guide. If fingers get cold, warm them in your pockets. Mittens don't work.

Colors and Fabrics Take a lesson from the birds and consider camouflage. The best way to get close to a bird or other wildlife is to blend in with the landscape and to approach quietly. Light colors such as white or yellow stand out amongst dark rocks and vegetation. Don't advertise your presence! Light colors do best on light sandy shores.

Another consideration is the fabric of your clothing. Nylon and some new "wonder fabrics" are practical in many ways, but some can be noisy. Think about walking with your arms at your sides. Do you hear a "zip, zip" sound? Sometimes this sound is annoying to hear and advertises your approach. Keep the noise factor in mind when making clothing selections. Soft fabrics are quietest.

Miscellany Birders often carry a field guide in a waist or shoulder bag. Some fanny-pack belts have a place for a water bottle, too. For long hikes, it's a good idea to carry a water bottle either in a pack or large pocket. Sunscreen, insect repellent, lip balm, and tissue can be tucked in a pocket. For wet, damp, or dirty terrain, a large plastic bag will protect your pants when you rest or sit to

The greater yellow legs is commonly seen in marshes and along shorelines.

observe birds. If weather conditions are wet, a zippered plastic bag can protect your binoculars, camera, or field guide. Study maps and carry a compass when birding in wilderness areas. It's a good idea to tell someone where you plan to go in case a search party is needed to find you. Carry a loud whistle (policeman or referee type) to summon emergency help.

Field Guides

Many good field guides are available in book stores. It's best to buy a current edition because bird names change as new species are discovered. You can choose from regional, national, and even continental field guides. Pick the ones that suit your birding activities.

A good field guide should include these things.

- *scientific names*
- *colored pictures showing both breeding and nonbreeding plumage (adult male, adult female, and immature bird)*
- *list of field marks, measurements, and voice*
- *behavior, habitat, and range*
- *checklists*

A field guide can be most helpful when birding. Record your sightings on the checklist at the back of the guide. Some birders prefer painted colored pictures of birds to photos, since they allow you to see markings more clearly.

When you're travelling, look for field guides for other regions of the world in book stores, museum gift shops, and natural history organizations. Just look around and choose what's best for you.

Where to Find Birds

You can see birds just about everywhere. Begin looking in yards or streets nearby. Some congregate in trees, while others busily feed on the ground. Bird feeders and birdbaths encourage more visitors.

Many species prefer special habitats. You'll find waterfowl, like

This American avocet is in winter plumage.

ducks, sandpipers, and herons, for example, in or near water. But bird populations often vary with the season and climate.

Joining a bird-watching group is a good way to get started. Associations, like the National Audubon Society in the United States or the Royal Society for the Protection of Birds in Great Britain, are quite active. These groups will help you learn what to look for and where to find it. Group outings are the fastest way to learn from more experienced eyes. When you repeat the same hikes, you'll be amazed at how easy it is to find and identify each species.

Visit a natural history museum to familiarize yourself with what a bird looks like close up. Zoos also have birds on display in aviaries. Check with local parks and recreation departments to locate a birding program in your community.

Bird sanctuaries, wildlife refuges, state parks, and nature preserves provide many opportunities for birdwatching. Ask other birders where they like to view birds. Return to these sites at different times of the year, and you'll probably discover different birds visiting.

Use the silhouette as a clue for identification.

The loggerhead shrike hunts in open and bushy areas.

When to See Birds

Knowing the best time of day for birding is important. Many birds are *crepuscular,* or active in early morning and late afternoon. So, that's the best time to view them. Owls are *nocturnal,* or active at night. Some birds are *diurnal,* or active during the day. Consult your field guide for full information.

The burrowing owl feeds on insects and small rodents.

Five Places to Look

- *Look in the trees and bushes.*
- *Check the areas where the landscape changes, such as the line between meadow and forest or water and shore.*
- *Check out high perching areas, like atop poles, high trees, and roofs.*
- *Observe bird feeders.*
- *Look in the sky to see flying birds and where they land.*

Also, with each season, the bird population changes. Depending on where you live, migration patterns may determine which birds are currently in the area.

Before venturing out for birding, take time to familiarize yourself with local birds. Using a field guide, check to find the kind of habitat the birds frequent, the color of their plumage, and the behavior they commonly exhibit.

Learn from the Pros

If possible, go birding with someone who has some expertise in bird identification, since that person will know where to look. Birding organizations usually like to share information, and local parks often have naturalists who offer tours or who can at least answer questions. In the United States, you could check with the U.S. Fish & Wildlife Service; in Canada, the Canadian Wildlife Service; in Great Britain, the Royal Society for the Protection of Birds; in Australia, the Royal Australian Ornithologists' Union; and in New Zealand, the Ornithological Society of New Zealand; or with the wildlife, natural history, or museum service in your community. Also consult the list of birding organizations and wildlife associations at the back of this book.

Hundreds of organizations and groups of various sizes are affiliated with bird-watching. Start with your local phone book and ask for suggestions from pros. It won't take long to find fellow birders who'd like to share this wonderful pastime.

Some communities, in addition, offer adult education classes in ornithology. Libraries, of course, have books on birds and birding and many have videotapes you can borrow. Birds, birders, and books about birds are everywhere.

Beginning birders learn from a naturalist.

Birding Etiquette

When you're on an outing with fellow birders, be consdierate of both humans and birds. There's nothing worse than a noisy, pushy, know-it-all dashing all opportunities of seeing the birds. These tips might help.

- *Ten people can't all be first when hiking on a 2½-foot-(75-cm-)wide trail. Take turns.*
- *When sighting a bird, refrain from bellowing, please. Try silently pointing or saying the bird's name in a modulated voice, about as loud as you'd use on the telephone. This may take great self-control when something rare or unexpected comes into view.*
- *If someone has a spotting scope and welcomes you to view through it, take turns and express your thanks for the privilege.*
- *Try not to one-up the leader.*
- *Give everyone a turn at identifying the birds. It's sad to think a new birder might miss an opportunity to participate because someone wants to hog the glory.*
- *Compliment the sharp eyes of someone who sees something and shares it. New birders thrive on positive reinforcement.*
- *Pick up your feet. Avoid making unnecessary noise.*
- *Never snap a branch back in someone's face. Help others by such obstacles.*
- *Help less agile folks over, under, around, and through fences.*
- *Leave the dog home.*
- *Small children or bored older people can make an outing just as miserable for everyone as it is for them.*
- *Remember to make rest stops before you go out in the wild, or simply plan your stops throughout the day.*
- *Avoid quibbling over an identification. If the bird has flown, and there's no way to prove your point; agree to disagree, and continue on.*
- *Protect the environment, and carry any trash you accumulate back home.*
- *Avoid bothering or inhibiting birds in any way, especially during nesting season.*
- *Leave the birdcall at home, unless you're invited to provide an expert demonstration. Let birds do it their way.*

Ring-necked pheasant

3

Bird Habitats— Where to Look

Habitat

The *habitat* is the place or type of site where a particular plant or animal lives and grows naturally. A good habitat provides food, water, protective cover or camouflage, and a safe environment for rearing offspring. Birds are found in many different habitats. Consult your field guide to learn the usual habitat of each bird you see.

Habitats are fairly easy to predict. Shorebirds, including swimmers and waders, will be found in or near water, at the shoreline or in marshlands. Perching birds who live in trees can be found in varied habitats. Fowllike birds usually dwell on the ground in bushy undergrowth that provides a good camouflage to protect them from predators. Birds of prey are found anywhere food is available. Large birds, such as eagles, can be found in open spaces that give room for free flight over large expanses of land and water. Aerialists, of course, are found in the air.

Some bird species have adapted to a variety of habitats. Many songbird species have adapted to human urbanization of what were once open woodlands and uncultivated places.

Range

Field guides show range maps that tell where a particular species of bird may regularly be seen. The abundance of these species varies throughout the birds' range, due to habitat, food supply, and other factors.

Birds stopping to feed or rest during migration are referred to as *visitors*. A bird seen on an irregular basis is considered a *casual visitor*. A *vagrant* has strayed from its usual migration path. Occasionally, a bird may be seen well out of the normal range for its species. Such rare sightings are referred to as *accidental* sightings. After a few seasons, you'll recognize resident birds.

Migration

Birds have adapted to harsh climate changes by moving with the temperature. Cold weather and less available food sends birds to warmer ranges, and as temperatures rise, birds return to their original habitat. This movement is called *migration*.

Most birds migrate when food supplies become scarce. They follow insects and flowering plant crops as seasons change and then return, often to the same neighborhood, when temperatures become warm again. Movement might be only a change of elevation from a mountain nesting site to a milder valley location a few miles or kilometres away in the winter, or at the other extreme, trans-equatorial migrations, that span continents and hemispheres.

Spectacular migrations of birds have long fascinated people. Avid birders await migrations just to see this multitude of birds in flight. It's possible to predict the arrival and departure of birds, since they vary little from year to year.

During migration, many species fly in groups or flocks that may number in the hundreds, even thousands, for some species. Their path or route is called a *flyway*. These aerial pathways follow coastlines, mountain ranges, river systems, and other natural land forms.

Scientists have thought that birds use various environmental clues to navigate their migration routes. At night the stars and the earth's magnetic field provide direction. During daylight, birds can follow visual

Good binoculars will help you identify the black-crowned night herons.

clues, such as land forms, coastlines, and mountain ranges, as well as the sun.

Migration distances vary depending on the species. Some birds, such as a woodpecker or a raven, may not migrate or may only move a short distance when seasons change. In contrast, the arctic tern flies 22,000 miles (35,200 km) in its annual migration from the Arctic and subarctic to coastal areas of Antarctica. Another species, the barn swallow, flies as far south as Brazil and Argentina each winter from Canada. Even delicate ruby-throated hummingbirds fly nonstop across the Gulf of Mexico from as far north as southern Canada to Mexico, Central America, and South America.

Birds and Nature Conservation

Human civilization has destroyed many natural habitats. For instance, we have logged forests and built whole cities where grassland once fed a multitude of species, and as a result, birds' populations have declined. Many species have altered their migratory patterns to adapt to this ever-changing landscape. Scientists have noted that the migratory songbird population has markedly declined. With the destruction of rain forests, birds have found it difficult to locate nesting sites and find abundant food sources.

Some migratory birds are gradually changing their winter ranges. House finches, for example, have adapted to human presence and to city environments. By taking advantage of gardens, bird feeders, and water in artificial ponds and bird baths, these birds have found ways to survive in cities during winter.

Amazing Migrants

How fast do migrating birds fly? This varies from species to species. In general, most birds fly between 20 and 50 miles (30 and 80 kilometres) per hour; a good tail wind could increase speed considerably.

Radar has been used to track many bird species. While most birds fly at an altitude of about 600 feet (180 metres), some small perching birds have been observed at about 10,000 feet (3,000 metres). The bar-headed goose can fly even higher. This species has been observed flying over the Himalayas at an altitude of over 32,800 feet (9,840 metres)!

Banding or Ringing

To track where birds go and to find out the population of each species, government wildlife agencies and a few private groups net and band a sampling of birds. These nets or traps are harmless and rarely injure the birds. Banding or ringing is practiced in wildlife refuges as well as lakes and rivers that serve as resting places for birds as they fly from one range to another.

The bird *band* or *ring* is a small metal strip with a coded number and the name and address of the agency responsible for banding. Someone carefully places this band or ring on the bird's leg and releases the bird so that it can resume migration.

Anyone finding a banded or ringed bird, whether it's dead or alive, should contact the agency and supply

When Is a Robin Not a Robin?

Early settlers in North America from the Old World mistakenly identified the red-breasted thrush (*Turdus migratorius*), which is 9 to 11 inches (22 to 28 cm) long, with the robin (*Erithacus rubecula*) found in England and Europe. This plump little European bird is only 5½ inches (14 cm) long. To differentiate between these two separate species, we refer to them by the common names American robin and robin or English robin.

American robin

English robin

M. DANZENBAKER

Bird banding or ringing can be done safely with special tools.

After the bird is weighed and examined, it's ready for release.

information about where and when the bird was found. If the bird is dead, sending the band or ring is also helpful. This information contributes to research and helps maintain an accurate census on bird populations.

Speckled mousebird

4

Bird
Identification

B irds come in all shapes, sizes, and colors, and that's why identifying them can be a real challenge. With a few simple observations, you can solve the mystery of what bird you've spotted.

Here's a guide for very basic identification. As you become more acquainted with birds, you'll be able to observe small details and field marks that identify subspecies. But to start, let's concentrate on these physical and behavioral features.

The Anna's hummingbird weighs less than an ounce.

Basic Guide

General Size First, familiarize yourself with three or four birds of different sizes to use as a guide. For example, a sparrow, a thrush, a duck, and a crane represent four short, full, or thin? Does the tail point upward like a wren or downwards like a robin? Is it pointed or squared off? Are the wings rounded or pointed when in flight?

The wild turkey can weigh several pounds or a few kilograms.

A bird's bill provides a clue about what it eats.

different body sizes. Decide which bird size is closest to the one you're trying to identify. You might describe the bird you're trying to identify as "larger than a sparrow" or "smaller than a thrush."

Basic Shape Next, note the body shape. Is it plump like a duck or slender as a swallow? Does it have a crest? What shape is the tail—long,

Bill Shape and Feeding Clues

Look at the bill. This gives you a clue about how the birds eats. A long thin bill is used for probing food by birds like sandpipers. Predators have a broad hooked bill as do eagles for tearing flesh. A duck's bill is wider than it is high and can be described as a filter. Insect eaters have slender pincerlike bills, while fish eaters, like the cormorant, have long, hooked tips. Seed eaters have short, stout bills, some strongly curved like a parrot's. Nectar feeders, such as hummingbirds, have long, thin bills for reaching into blossoms. Vultures like most scavengers have a strong hooked bill for opening carcasses. Pelicans have a pouch for scooping food from water.

The owl has a bill for tearing flesh.

Feet Notice adaptations of the feet. Predators have talons for gripping that are not suitable for walking. Aquatic birds have webbed feet to help them propel through water more efficiently. Two toes in front and two toes in back of a woodpecker's foot aid in walking up tree trunks.

Perching birds have three toes facing forward and one toe in back. When walking, the toes spread out, but when on a branch, tendons in the bird's leg make the toes curl, which keep it from falling while asleep.

A long bill is used for probing.

Legs Notice the legs—are they long or short? Are they covered with feathers like an owl's or are they bare like a robin's? Do you see the legs when the bird is in flight?

Color At first sight, what is the main color you see? Look closer to

Perching birds have grasping feet.

see if there's a difference in the color of the cap, belly, rump, back, wings, or tail. It can be tricky to see details, but the largest areas of color should be easy to identify. As you become more experienced at bird identification, you will be able to pick out more details.

Birds can vary in color between sexes and also during the breeding season. Males tend to be more colorful than females and juveniles.

Behavior Watch the bird to see if it has an unusual behavior, such as head bobbing, wing flapping, or courting displays. Does the bird perch in trees, feed on the ground, swim or dive in water? Is the bird a loner or does it stay in a group or flock? These observations provide clues to the bird's identity.

How a bird flies also offers clues. Does it flap its wings rapidly and then glide, or are the wing beats rhythmic? Is the flight pattern in a straight line, or does it dip between wing flapping?

When does the bird feed—morning, evening, or all the time? What preening habits does it display? Is the bird territorial or does it stay with a flock? Is there courtship behavior? You'll find answers to all

these questions as you become accustomed to observing birds.

A bird's language includes both auditory displays (sounds) and visual displays (body movement and positions). Observing these interactions can be an exciting aspect of bird-watching.

Birds of prey have talons for killing.

Field Marks Each species of bird has its own *field marks*. These identifying details include wing bars, color patches, color bands, shapes of body parts, and more. Consult your field guide for the field marks that distinguish one species of bird from others.

PARTS OF A BIRD

eye
crown
earpatch
eyebrow
lore
eye ring
bill
throat
wingbars
shoulder
(scapular)
wing
breast
upper tail coverts
tail
belly
secondaries
leg
primaries
outer tail feathers
tarsus

Computer Graphics by DAN LLOYD

Voice Listen to the bird's song. Does it warble, screech, or repeat the same note over and over? Every bird has its own special way of singing. Some call their name, like the killdeer and chickadee, while the towhee sings "drink your teee, drink your teee." Veteran birders often locate the bird by its voice before making a visual sighting. This skill comes with experience.

Some birds have a joint call between mates. The male Canada goose gives a two-syllable "a-honk" sound and the female returns a "hink" call. These sounds are made alternately so that it sounds as if it's coming from only one bird.

There are many good audio tapes for learning bird songs, usually sold where field guides are sold. Also check your local library to see if some are available. Concentrate on birds you're most likely to encounter.

Scientific Names

Generally, amateur bird-watchers only need to learn the common name for each bird species. Use of the scientific or Latin name is usually only necessary for scientific research or for birders who converse with people from foreign countries. The scientific name for each bird represents its classification into relatively small categories. All birds belong to the *class Aves*. This large category is divided into *orders*, which are in turn divided into still smaller groups called *families*. And these families are made up of different *genera*, which consist of different *species*.

The scientific name for the red-winged blackbird, for instance, is *Agelaius phoeniceus*. The first term, *Agelaius*, indicates the genus, and the second term, *phoeniceus*, indicates the species. Note that the first term is capitalized and the second is not. These Latin names are usually presented in italics (or underlined, since underlining signals italics).

Starting Out

Birding takes time and patience; so, don't get frustrated about not being able to identify each bird immediately. The beginning birder need not be too concerned with more than just identifying the general species of bird rather than with a more technical observation. As you become more experienced, it will become second nature for you to see subtle details and more specific identification will become easier.

Consider location or geography of each species. Experienced birders usually do their homework before going outdoors. First, they consult a checklist of birds common to the area. There's no use looking for a swan in a tree. Learn which birds you'll probably encounter. (See chapter 5 for descriptions of common birds.)

Bird Categories

Roger Tory Peterson, recognized as a leading authority in birding, has written field guides that have been the standard for bird identification since the early 1940s. To make comparisons, he divided the bird world into these eight categories.

- *Swimmers—ducks, ducklike birds*
- *Aerialists—terns, gulls*
- *Waders with long legs— herons, cranes, egrets, bitterns*
- *Waders with short legs— sandpipers, plovers, curlews*

- *Fowllike birds—pheasant, grouse, chickenlike birds*
- *Birds of prey—hawks, eagles, owls, kites*
- *Passerine (perching birds)— robins, finches, sparrows, warblers*
- *Miscellaneous nonpasserine— hummingbirds, woodpeckers, kingfishers, cuckoos*

Learn the general characteristics of each group, and you'll be well on your way to quick identification of the families and species of basic bird groups.

Then, make a mental checklist of these questions.

- *To which group does the bird belong?*
- *Does the bird have any distinguishing field marks, such as stripes, wing bars, rings around the eyes, or color patches?*
- *Does the bird have an unusual crest or crown?*
- *Can you observe any unusual behavior?*
- *What kind of vocalization does the bird make?*
- *What kind of feet and bill does the bird have?*

By process of elimination and the aid of a field guide, you should be able to find the identity of a particular bird.

Bird Lists

Birders are great list makers. These checklists record sightings of birds identified. It's fun to record how many different species you've seen and where you've seen them. Birders often have several lists in progress. These could be a yearly list, trip list, yard list, city list, or life list. With approximately 8,600 species worldwide, your list(s) could be long.

These lists serve another purpose besides one's own enjoyment. They help check trends in bird populations and can serve as a record for local, regional, or national surveys.

Local Audubon and other birding societies, and state, provincial, regional, and national park services or local birding clubs probably have lists of birds that can be seen in their area. In addition to these lists, birding associations offer an up-to-date listing of all birds currently identified in their continent.

Most field guides have a checklist of species in the index. This provides

Cattle egrets originated in the Old World and slowly expanded
their range around the world.

a handy way to keep track of your sightings. Don't forget to take a pencil and small notepad along when you go birding. Here are basic guidelines for making a list.

- *Record only positive identifications.*
- *Birds must be wild—no zoo or caged birds.*
- *Birds must be alive.*

Ruby-crowned kinglet

Townsend's warbler

California clapper rail

Jungle fowl

Field Mark Quiz

Look at the illustration and try to use what you've learned about field marks. Which group of birds would it be in? What are the distinguishing characteristics of the head, bill, neck, body, legs, and feet? Turn to a field guide to find the correct identity.

If you guessed the roseate spoonbill, you're absolutely right!

Rare Bird Alert

In conjunction with lists, several birding hot lines keep avid bird-watchers informed through a re-corded phone message about the lat-est sightings of rare birds, or birds out of their normal range. Consult your local birding society for infor-mation on hot lines.

Rare birds appear when you least ex-pect them.

Song sparrow

5

Birds Near
and Far

After learning the basics of bird-watching, you'll discover a new awareness of birds. When you hear a song, your eyes will automatically search for the sound's source. Eventually, it will become second nature to scan outdoor surroundings for birds.

When travelling, you'll find ample opportunities to see new and familiar species. Remember, birds fly; migration takes them great distances throughout the year. Birds have also been introduced from other countries. Another factor is the change, more often expansion, of a traditional range of a species. With the devastation of nesting sites in rain forests, many birds are adapting to different habitats for nesting. Unusual birds that have escaped aviaries and that have adapted to a totally new environment have also been sighted.

Birds in this chapter are arranged in conventional categories—swimmers, aerialists, long-legged waders, short-legged waders, fowllike birds, birds of prey, passerine (perching birds), and miscellaneous nonpasserine. Habitat, field marks, behavior, and seasonal movement of common birds you're likely to encounter precede photos of birds from these groups found around the world. First learn to identify these common birds and their usual environment, and you'll find it easier to recognize other birds from the same category and similar species.

Birds from regions as diverse as Iceland, eastern Africa, China, Australia, and South America are identified by common name and range or location. These groups of birds have certain features in common and may be found in similar habitats. Remember, swimmers and waders, as the titles of these groups suggest, are usually found in or near water.

Long-legged waders, like herons, ibises, storks, and flamingos, feed where fish and other aquatic life are plentiful. Some storks, however, also feed on carrion. Fowllike birds may be found on the ground in grassy or wooded areas. Day-flying birds of prey, like falcons, hawks, eagles, kites, buzzards, and vultures, choose a high precipice or tree branch from which to spot prey. They also need open space, and you may also see them circling in the sky above likely prey. Night-flying birds of prey, like owls, goatsuckers, and swifts, may be hard to locate in the daytime.

The barn swallow is quick in flight and darts to catch flying insects.

Passerine, or perching birds, are the most advanced and successful group of living birds, with over 5,000 of the 8,600 species of birds worldwide. They may be found perched on trees, fences, and telephone wires. Both songbirds and the more primitive non-songbirds make up this group. Most songbirds, like larks, swallows, thrushes, titmice, wrens, flycatchers, orioles, and finches, are small. The raven is the giant among passerine.

Nonpasserine includes a miscellany of birds. Some, like pigeons, have adapted to urban environments—nesting on cornices and windowsills and gathering on sidewalks and in parks. Woodpeckers are found on tree trunks, including those of dead trees, while pelicans fish near shores of lakes and oceans.

When you travel, use a field guide for the region, country, or continent you're visiting. Note the seasonal movement of each species. You may also observe these "foreign" birds in aviaries. You could schedule a visit to an aviary as preparation for the field or as an enjoyment in itself. But part of the fun and adventure of birding is discovering birds in their native environment, with your own ears, eyes, and binoculars.

CANADA GOOSE
Branta canadensis
L 25–45 in (63–114 cm) /
W 50–68 in (127–173 cm)

Habitat: Near coastal marshes and lake shores.

Field Marks: The Canada goose has a black head and neck with broad, white cheek or chin strap. Wings are dark and white coverts are under the tail. The bill and legs are black. Several subspecies have varied size and coloration from tan to brown. Males and females have the same plumage.

Behavior: The Canada goose has many displays easy to interpret. When the head and neck are extended forward, the goose is giving a threat and will probably attack. This behavior is common during breeding and when establishing territory. The bird may pump its head up and down or rhythmically dip its neck into the water during courtship. The male makes the sound "a-honk." Females give a "hink" call that alternates with the male's vocalization. When greeting each other, the pair sounds like "a-honk, hink, a-honk, hink." Pairs mate for life. Canada geese usually have a territory about ¼ to 1 acre (.1 to .4 hectare) in size. The male defends the nest site until the young have hatched. Nests are built on the ground, near water. Usually five eggs are in a clutch.

Seasonal Movement: Geese migrate south in the fall and north in the spring. Flocks fly in a V-shaped formation or in long lines.

MALLARD DUCK (WILD DUCK)

Anas platyrhynchos

L 16–23 in (40–58 cm)

Habitat: Ponds, marshes, grain fields, irrigated land.

Field Marks: *Male*—shiny green head, white collar, grayish to chestnut brown breast, white tail with curl in center feathers. Bright violet blue speculum bordered in white; orange feet, yellowish bill. *Female*—brown mottled body, whitish tail, orange feet, bill dark with orange patches. The speculum is bright violet blue with white borders.

Behavior: Only females make quacking sounds, and males make a short whistle call and a nasal "rhaeb" or "yeeb." Pairing takes place during fall and early spring. Competitive courting occurs as two or more males display in the presence of a female. Pair formation involves head shaking and tail shaking behavior. The female follows the male while repeatedly flicking her bill to one side of her body. She vocalizes a "quegegegegege" sound to excite her mate. Head pumping by rhythmically lifting heads up and down as they face each other is usually followed by mating. A nest is built near water in early spring. Eight to ten eggs are in a clutch. The male defends the small territory of open water and reeds, about ⅛ to ¼ acre (.05 to .1 hectare) in size. This area is separate but near the nesting site. Mallards have the ability to take off almost vertically from the water.

Seasonal Movement: Mallards usually fly southward for the winter and northward in the spring. Some, however, remain in the north during cold weather if there is sufficient food and open water.

AMERICAN COOT
(MUDHEN)
Fulica americana
L 13–15½ in (33–38 cm)

Habitat: Marshes, lakes, ponds, wetlands (saltwater or freshwater).

Field Marks: The American coot's body is plump and ducklike; plumage slate gray with a darker head; wings have a white edge. Bill and shield on the forehead are white; legs and feet greenish; a white patch appears under a short tail; toes lobed; eyes red. Juveniles have lighter coloring.

Behavior: Coots are ducklike in many ways. They dive similarly and also dabble or tip up in shallow water. Coots swim with ducks and feed on the food stirred up by the ducks' webbed feet. When swimming, coots make a pumping motion with their heads. Take-off from the water involves running and flapping wings vigorously to become airborne. When in flight, they usually go no higher than 15 feet (5 m) from the ground. Courtship displays include the male chasing the female across the water. Vocalizations are "kuk-kuk-kuk" between pairs. They also make short, rough notes that sound like grunts, croaks, and whistles, both day and night. Nests are built out of stems of marsh plants that float on water in freshwater marshes, lakes, ponds, or wetlands. This nest is anchored by other plants which also conceal its location. Usually two to twenty-two eggs are in a clutch. Both male and female incubate

the eggs. Chicks are able to care for themselves within seven to eight weeks after hatching. Coots gather together in large flocks.

Seasonal Movement: American coots cover a large range which includes most of the United States year-round. Some birds fly north to Canada for breeding and return south when the weather turns cold. Other birds stay in warm climates as year-round residents.

WESTERN GREBE, *west coast of United States*

COMMON LOON, *Canada, coasts of North America*

Birds Near and Far **59**

PIED-BILLED GREBE, *North America, Central America*

MAGPIE GOOSE,
Australia

MOORHEN,
*England, Europe,
North America,
Australia*

PLUMED DUCK,
Australia

SHELDUCK,
Australia

WOOD DUCK,
North America

CAPE BARREN GOOSE, *Australia*

BLACK SWAN AND CYGNET, *New Zealand*

WHOOPER SWAN, *northern Europe, China, Iceland*

Northern Pintail,
northern hemisphere

Chestnut Teal,
Australia

Pacific Black Duck,
New Zealand, Australia

RING-BILLED GULL

Larus delawarensis

L 18–20 in (45–51 cm)

Habitat: Seacoasts, parks, fields, garbage dumps, lakes.

Field Marks: Plumage is mostly white with gray wings and back; wings are long and narrow; wing tips are black with white dots; the sharp bill is yellow with a black ring; toes are webbed; legs and feet are yellowish green; head streaked with brown in winter. Juvenile gulls have mottled brown plumage. It takes three years to attain adult coloration.

Behavior: Gulls are known for their ability to eat just about anything. They are welcomed by farmers who are plagued with grasshoppers and other destructive insects as well as small rodents. They also eat fish and are known to scavenge at dumps. Gulls move about in flocks, but they will pair off in breeding season. Breeding colonies may be quite large. Usually gulls pick a safe location to nest on islands and shores of freshwater lakes. Displays include head tossing in which the gull flips its bill upward repeatedly, then draws the head in. This display is seen prior to mating or it may lead to mate feeding. During courtship and mating, gulls have a distinctive three-part call which sounds like "ow-ow-ow, kee-kee-kee, kyowkyowkyow." When pairs lower their bodies and tip forward in a pecking manner, this is recognized as a choking display. The behavior could be to establish territory, initiate courtship, or promote nest building. Gulls make a "huoh-huoh-huoh-houh" call accompanying this display. Alarm calls like a series of short notes "gagagaga, gagagaga" given when danger is near. Nests built on the ground are lined with grass and stems. Usually two to four eggs are in a clutch. Chicks swim at an early age to escape predators. Gulls have long periods of resting or preening. They like to sit high on posts for safety and to get a good view of their surroundings. Gulls are somewhat unafraid of humans and may become aggressive if they see food to their liking.

Seasonal Movement: Gulls initiate a northward migration in the spring. In the fall and winter these gulls fly to warmer climates throughout the United States and Mexico as well as in western and northern Europe.

SILVER GULLS, *Australia, New Zealand, Pacific region*

HERRING GULL, *North American coasts*

© J. DELEVORYAS

FORSTER'S TERN, *North America*

PACIFIC GULL,
southern hemisphere

BLACK-HEADED GULL,
Europe,
Iceland, England

CRESTED TERN,
Australia

GREAT BLUE HERON (BLUE CRANE)
Ardea herondias
L 46–54 in (116–137 cm)

Habitat: Wetlands, marshes, tidal flats, and shorelines in either freshwater or saltwater.

Field Marks: The great blue heron is one of the largest members of the heron family. Plumage is gray blue with black stripe that extends above the eye. The head and neck are white with a black foreneck, and occasionally a cinnamon color on the neck. The bill is long, dagger-shaped, and yellow. Legs are long, yellowish; thighs are chestnut; and feet have long toes. The wingspan is in excess of 6 feet (2 m). Both male and female have the same plumage. There is also a great white heron found only in Florida.

© J. DELEVORYAS

Behavior: The great blue heron can be seen motionless in shallow water as it hunts for food. It stands either with head erect or with the head held between its shoulders. Prey consists of small animals, such as fish, snakes, insects, frogs, and smaller birds, living in or near water. Long legs help the heron catch fish in deeper water. When alarmed, the bird gives a series of loud, hoarse "grak, grak, grak" squawks or croaks. In flight, the heron folds its neck back toward its body and extends its legs backwards.

At the onset of breeding season, the male takes over an old nest. When a female approaches the nest, he displays by ruffling breast feathers while lifting and lowering his neck. Nests built of sticks rest high in a tree or on a ledge. When the pair meets at the nest, they perform a greeting ceremony by lifting the head and neck feathers and emitting a sequence of guttural cries. A clutch consists of three to seven eggs, usually four, which are incubated by both parents. After hatching, both parents take turns feeding and guarding the chicks. Pairs only stay together for one breeding season and rearing the brood.

Heron colonies are called "heronries" or "rookeries." Often several herons nest in the same tree or nearby.

Seasonal Movement: Great blue herons migrate to ranges as far north as Alaska and northern Canada in the spring and return to warmer climates as far south as Mexico, the Galápagos Islands, and the West Indies in winter. This bird is widespread in North America.

C. NEWMAN

AMERICAN BITTERN, *North America*

CATTLE EGRET

all continents except Antarctica

MARABOU STORK, *Africa*

GLOSSY IBIS, *Europe*

C. NEWMAN

GREEN-BACKED HERON, *North America*

J. SILLIMAN

BUFF-NECKED IBIS, *South America*

AUSTRALIAN BUSTARD,
Australia

COMMON CRANES' GREETING RITUAL,
North America

BLACK-CROWNED NIGHT HERON, *North America*

SNOWY EGRET, *North America, South America*

CHILEAN FLAMINGO, *South America*

EMU, *Australia*

KILLDEER
Charadrius vociferus
L 9–11 in (22–28 cm)

Habitat: Open spaces, tidelands, riverbanks, pastures.

Field Marks: A member of the plover family, the killdeer has a brown back, white underside, and a breast with two distinctive black bands. Its rump is reddish orange, seen in flight; wings have a white stripe and dark edge; the tail is rounded, with a black band, tipped in white. The killdeer has a white eyebrow with black band on the forehead, yellowish legs, and a slender, black bill. Fuzzy chicks have similar coloring but just one breast band as do other plovers.

Behavior: Known for its call, "killdeeh-killdee," killdeer are usually seen in small flocks or individually. The killdeer makes short runs and then stops to listen, look, and peck at the ground. Farmers see them during cultivation when insects, grubs, and beetles are turned up by plows. They are also known to eat small crabs, crayfishes, and snails. Males fly in a high, circling pattern using a slow wing beat while calling. Scientists consider this a courtship behavior.

Killdeer build nests on the ground in a slight depression of pebbles lined with grasses. Three to five eggs are in a clutch. Chicks fledge twenty-five days after hatching. When they sense danger, adult killdeers give a "tttttrrrrrrrrr" alarm. The head may bob up and down. Chicks sometimes freeze their movement and close their eyes. If parents fear the nest will be discovered, they use the ploy of a wounded bird by dragging a wing on the ground as though crippled. Another way chicks escape is to go to water and swim or even dive underwater to avoid detection. Killdeers defend a territory of about an acre (.4 hectare) for the duration of courtship to the end of the breeding period.

Season Movement: Found throughout the northern hemisphere, killdeers migrate to warmer climates as far as South America in the winter and return to North America in early spring.

AMERICAN AVOCET, *North America*

VIRGINIA RAIL, *North America*

RED-NECKED PHALAROPE, *Arctic Circle, Africa, South America, Europe*

BLACK-WINGED STILT, *Australia*

BLACK-NECKED STILT, *North America*

SHORE BIRDS, *North America*

RUDDY TURNSTONE, *North America, Europe*

DOWITCHER, *North America*

MARBLED GODWIT, *North America*

RED PHALAROPE, *North America, South America, Africa, Arctic Circle*

RING-NECKED PHEASANT

Phasianus colchicus

L 30–36 in (76–92 cm) males;
20–25 in (50–63 cm) females

Species Note: The ring-necked pheasant was introduced to North America from Asia.

Habitat: Fields, brushy undergrowth, open country.

Field Marks: Ring-necked pheasants have a large body, the size of a chicken. Males have iridescent plumage. The head and neck are greenish or sometimes purple; a white collar at the base of the neck separates the bronze, black, and brown mottled feathers. The red eye patch and cheeks are bare skin. The tail is long and tapered, ending in a point. Males have a spur on each foot. Females are smaller with dull brown mottled plumage with a long, tapered pointed tail. Both sexes have yellow seed-eater bills. Wings are short and rounded.

Behavior: Pheasants are strong fliers for short distances. When flushed, the male flaps his wings noisily and gives a harsh croaking sound of "cucket-cucket." Females give an alarm call of "queep-queep." When hunted, pheasants often run on the ground through thick undergrowth to avoid detection. They have the ability to take off into flight almost upward. Flight can be almost silent. Pheasants feed shortly after sunrise on seeds, grain, insects, berries, or other plant materials. In the spring, males court females by crowing a "kork-kok" or "kock-kack" call, followed by a flapping of wings. They defend a territory of a few acres or a hectare from other males. A successful male attracts and mates with two to four females. They build nests scraped out from the ground, and lined with grasses and weeds, in the male's crowing territory. Usually ten to twelve eggs are laid. Females may build nests near other nests in the male's territory. When danger threatens the nest of chicks, the female lures the predator away with a crippled bird act.

Seasonal Movement: Pheasants gather in large flocks in the fall and feed in grain fields. In the winter, they seek safety from the cold by hiding in the entrance of woodchuck burrows or other natural shelters. When spring arrives, flocks break up and males establish territories which usually range about 1–2 miles (1.6–3.2 km).

Peacock (Peafowl), *India (introduced worldwide)*

Peacock (Peafowl), *India (introduced worldwide)*

Jungle Fowl, *Asia*

Peahen and Chick (Peafowl), *India (introduced worldwide)*

WILD TURKEY, *North America*

GUINEA FOWL, *Africa*

BUTTON QUAIL, *Japan*

SCALED QUAIL, *southern United States, Mexico*

LADY AMHERST'S PHEASANT, *China*

SILVER PHEASANT, *southwestern Asia*

YELLOW-NECKED SPUR FOWL, *Africa*

REEVE'S PHEASANT, *China*

ELLIOT'S PHEASANT, *China*

GOLDEN PHEASANT, *China*

BOBWHITE, *North America*

BALD EAGLE

Haliaeëtus leucocephalus

L 30–43 in (76–110 cm)

Habitat: Rivers, lakes, seacoasts.

Field Marks: The adult is blackish brown with white head and tail feathers. The term *bald* means "streaked or marked with white." Feet are yellow with powerful talons; legs are feathered halfway to the feet, the beak is yellow and hooked for tearing prey, and the wingspread is 6 to 8 feet (182 to 244 cm). Immature birds are brown with blotchy white on the underwing.

Behavior: Bald eagles are known for spectacular courtship flights. The male dives swiftly at the female and touches her lightly on the back. Sometimes, while midair, both touch feet and tumble over and over. Nests, usually built high in trees or on rocky ledges, are constructed with sticks and lined with mosses, pine needles, and feathers. Over several years, eagles add more sticks to the nest. It isn't uncommon for a nest to measure more than 7 feet (214 cm) across. Usually two eggs are laid. Chicks fledge about seventy-two to seventy-five days after hatching. The bald eagle has a territory of about 2 to 3 miles (3 to 5 km) depending on how much food is available. They often sit high on a tree for hours waiting for prey to come into view. In the northwestern United States, bald eagles gather in large groups when salmon are running in rivers. These fish are easy prey for hungry birds. Flight is characterized as gliding or soaring. Wings are kept flat. An eagle has acute vision and can see a distance of about 2 miles (3 to 4 km) while soaring in the air. When the eagle spots prey, the bird dives and grabs it with strong, sharp talons.

Seasonal Migration: Bald eagles that reside in the far northern regions of Alaska and Canada migrate south to warmer climates in winter.

GREAT HORNED OWL
Bubo virginianus
L 18–25 in (45–64 cm)

Habitat: Wooded areas, chaparral, open country, deserts, canyons, cliffs, suburbs.

Field Marks: The great horned owl has a large and powerful, stocky body and a wingspan between 36 and 60 inches (90 and 155 cm). Its plumage is brown, spotted with a darker brown barred pattern, eyes are yellow, and eyesight is acute even in darkness. Throat feathers are white, ear tufts widely spaced, and it has a sharp, hooked beak. The female is larger than the male.

Behavior: The hearing is acute. This nocturnal hunter roosts in trees during the day. If discovered by flocks of smaller birds, the owl may be mobbed and fly to safety. It flies silently and catches any prey available such as mice, rabbits, grouse, frogs, fish, and small birds with its powerful claws, called talons. The owl has a feeding site where it brings its prey and which it tears into large pieces and swallows whole. Undigestible parts, such as fur, feathers, or bones, are regurgitated as pellets. Courtship displays include the male and female hooting at each other. Breeding occurs in isolation away from other birds. Nests located high up in a tree are usually those abandoned by red-tailed hawks, eagles, crows, or squirrels. Usually two to three eggs are in a clutch. The great horned owl makes territorial calls in a series of four to seven hoots. These deep, muffled hoots may be heard for great distances.

Seasonal Movement: Great horned owls do not make migrations of any great distance. In extremely cold areas in winter, they commonly fly to warmer climates. These owls range from the furthest northern regions of North America to the most southern tip of South America.

AMERICAN KESTREL (SPARROW HAWK)
Falco sparverius
L 8–10½ in (20–27 cm) (female larger)

Species Note: In Europe, Asia, and North Africa, a similar species is the *Falco tinnunculus*.

Habitat: Open country, cities.

Field Marks: The American kestrel is the smallest of falcons. The back and tail are rust colored; cheeks are white with two black stripes, sometimes referred to as moustache; and the head gray with rufus crown patches. Males have blue gray wing coverts; females are rufus. Legs are yellowish. When in flight, a trailing edge of translucent spots is visible on the wings. The bill is dark and hooked, the iris of eye is dark brown with cere, and the eye ring is yellow. Leg feathers are white to rufus, the belly is white with black spots, and the tail has a black band.

Behavior: The American kestrel is frequently seen hovering above prey or perched on high poles, wires, or treetops. From this viewpoint, the kestrel can spot prey, like rodents, lizards, snakes, small birds, and insects. Flight can be direct with rapid wing beats for short distances, then gliding or soaring and hovering. If the kestrel locates prey, it partially folds its wings, swooping down to grasp the prey with its deadly talons. It then flies to a perch and eats large prey while holding it under both feet. When alarmed, it raises and lowers its tail and screams, "killy-killy-killy." Kestrels are solitary birds. Territories range from 100 acres (40 hectares) for nonbreeding, hunting areas to 250 acres (100 hectares) for breeding in summer. Courtship involves the female giving a whine call that tells the male she is receptive. The male flies directly to the female's back, and she moves her tail to one side for mating. Mating may take place several times a day for a period of several weeks. A nest is a tree cavity, unlined. The female lays three to four eggs. She incubates them while the male hunts for food. When mate feeding occurs, the male calls to his mate and she flies to him. A display of head bobbing follows the exchange of food. The female then takes the food to another perch and consumes it. The male resumes hunting.

Seasonal Movement: The American kestrel and other similar species of kestrel have varied patterns of movement due to their large range throughout North America, Europe, Asia, Australia, and Africa. Birds in the northern regions migrate south to warmer climates in winter. Those birds that have territories in warmer regions may stay year-round in the same location if food is available.

TURKEY VULTURE, *North America*

YELLOW-HEADED VULTURE, *South America*

J. SILLIMAN

OSPREY, *North America, Europe, Africa*

BLACK-SHOULDERED KITE, *North America*

NANKING KESTREL, *Australia*

Andean Condor, *South America*

GOLDEN EAGLE,
Europe, North Africa, Asia,
North America

GREAT HORNED OWL, *North America*

BURROWING OWL,
North America

J. SILLIMAN

**LONG-EARED
OWL,** *North America,
Europe, Asia*

J. SILLIMAN

BARN OWL,
*worldwide except
Antarctica*

SWAINSON'S HAWK (DARK PHASE),
North America

SENSE OF SMELL This little known fact will certainly dispel a notion you may have held since childhood. You've probably been told, "If you find a baby bird on the ground, don't pick it up because the parent will smell a human scent and reject the offspring." This isn't true. Most birds, especially songbirds, have tiny olfactory lobes in the brain. Their sense of smell is marginal at best and plays little or no part in their lives.

Ducks, however, have a somewhat more developed sense of smell. Still more developed are geese, emus, and sea birds, like albatrosses and shearwaters. The kiwi of New Zealand has a higher sense of smell, which it uses to find underground earthworms. This seems to compensate for the kiwi's relatively poor eyesight.

The vulture family, like other birds of prey, has a more highly developed olfactory sense. This enables vultures to first find carrion by the scent of the rotting carcass, then by eyesight.

BARN SWALLOW
Hirundo rustica
L 6–7½ in (15–45 cm)

Habitat: Large open areas with sparse or low vegetation; nests under the caves of buildings, bridges, or other structures created by humans.

Field Marks: This is the only North American swallow with a truly forked tail. Plumage includes blue black backs with a reddish brown throat, buffy to cinnamon undersides, and whitish spots on a long tail. Its wings are pointed. Both male and female have the same coloration.

Behavior: Swallows are graceful in flight and feed on flying insects as they soar and dive over open farmland. Flight is fast and often close to the ground or water. Territories are usually the space between the nest and the nearest perch. When in close quarters, neighboring birds respect each other's territories. If an intruder comes into the territory, it is usually met by an attack and a chase. During courtship pairs fly high in the air.

The male chases the female and sings a "twitter" song. He also sings the song while perched. Females return a "stutter" call. Barn swallows build nests of mud, horse hair, grasses, and feathers under a shelter, such as a barn roof or bridge supports. Several dozen birds nest near each other, which restricts their territories. Usually five eggs are in a clutch, and there are one or two broods a year. After the chicks have fledged, they form flocks and perch together. Families tend to stay together for a few weeks after leaving the nest. It is not uncommon to see several dozen swallows perched together on a telephone wire or wire fence.

Seasonal Movement: Barn swallows migrate at the end of summer to warmer climates in Central America, Mexico, Florida, or the West Indies. In early spring they return to their nesting areas, which might be anywhere in the United States, or farther north even to northern Canada, Europe, or Asia. Swallows are found on all continents except Antarctica.

AMERICAN ROBIN
Turdus migratorius
L 9–11 in (22–28 cm)

Habitat: Woodlands, suburbs, swamps.
Field Marks: The American robin has a gray brown upper body and reddish orange breast (males have more intense color). The head and tail are darker brown tipped in white. The lower belly is off-white, the bill yellow, and three white broken lines are around the eye. Juveniles have a speckled breast, gray back, and rusty underparts.
Behavior: A member of the thrush family, the American robin is abundant throughout North America. It can be seen as far south as southern Mexico. During the winter huge flocks roost together and feed en masse on worms, insects, and berries. When in flight or communal roosting, robins make an "eeeee-eeeee" call similar to that of a cedar waxwing. As mating occurs, flocks disperse and only males roost together in small groups while females incubate the eggs. Territories are not clearly defined, but they are approximately ⅓ acre (.14 hectare). Both male and female defend the territory. Birds give a "tuk-tuk" or "teek-teek" call and repeatedly flick the tail to signal danger. When alarmed or attacking, the bird runs with its tail at a 45-degree angle and its head lowered. A series of short runs toward an opponent eventually moves it to another area. This behavior is common on lawns or feeding

areas. Nests are built in trees or a building structure. Nest materials are grasses and mud. A clutch usually has three or four eggs and usually two or three broods a year. Males return to the same area to breed year after year.
Seasonal Movement: Robins gather in large flocks to make their winter migration to warmer southern climates. If food, such as berries, is available, some birds remain in colder climates.

COMMON CROW
Corvus brachyrhynchos
L 17–18 in (43–46 cm)

Species Note: A similar northern European species is the carrion crow, *Corvus corone corone*.

Habitat: Open and wooded country; abundant throughout North America in varying habitats.

Field Marks: The crow is black over its entire body; in bright light, the feathers have a metallic, glossy sheen. Eyes are brown, the tail is fan-shaped, and the bill long and heavy but smaller than a raven's.

Behavior: In the fall, huge flocks often fly to farmlands to feed on corn or grain. They are also fond of insects. Owls and hawks may be mobbed or harassed by flocks of crows. The crow eats a large variety of food, anything from insects, small crustaceans, farm crops, bird's eggs, and fruit to carrion. They have even been known to rob chicks from other bird's nests. Undigested materials are regurgitated as pellets. In the spring, crows break into small groups which consist of the breeding pair and their nonbreeding offspring from the previous year. At this time crows are secretive and go about nest building, egg laying, and incubation quietly. They build nests high in trees out of sticks, twigs, grasses, shredded bark, moss, string, or other soft materials. Courtship includes head bobbing with wings and tail feathers slightly spread. The crows give a "rattle" call which at times is almost like a "coo" sound. Courtship displays are usually seen in the morning. During this time, territory around the immediate area of the nest is defended by the adult pair and the offspring from the last year's brood. They chase other crows away until the new brood has fledged. Crows have one or two broods a year of four or five chicks. Adult pairs may return to the same nesting site two or three years in a row. Their offspring do not reach sexual maturity until they are two years old. After the fledging of young, crows again form large flocks and roost in large numbers. They fly in predictable routes to reach these communal roosts.

Seasonal Migration: Migration patterns vary. Those birds inhabiting the far north fly considerable distances south in winter, and those living in warm climates stay in the same location. Flocks move around a general area to locate where the food supply is plentiful.

CHICKADEE FAMILY
Paridae
L 4¾–5¾ in (12–15 cm)

Species Note: There are six species of chickadee in North America; all species have the same general characteristics.

Habitat: Forests, woodland groves, or in suburbs in trees and shrubs.

Field Marks: The chickadee is a member of the titmouse family. Characteristics include an upper body and tail that are light gray, a white underbody, black cap and bib, and white cheeks. Wing coverts and secondary feathers on wings are edged in white.

Behavior: These hardy birds have a structured and predictable behavior. They keep two territories, one for breeding and one for nonbreeding, which is defended by the flock. Breeding territories cover approximately 10 acres (4 hectares). Males establish territories in late winter or early spring. They give a "free-bee" song as the breeding phase progresses. Males chase each other and their songs declare their territory. Courtship includes wing quivering as wings are lowered and body assumes a crouched position. Pairs break away from the flock and begin feeding on their own. The mated pair builds a nest by digging a hole on a rotted tree branch or by occupying an abandoned woodpecker hole. The nest is lined with moss, plant fibres, hair, feathers, and other soft materials. A clutch of six eggs is laid; offspring fledge in about four weeks. Flocks begin to form again in late summer after one or two broods have fledged. At this time they frequently give the familiar "chickadee-dee" call. They use a "tseet-tseet" call often while feeding. When danger is near, a "see-see-see-see" call is given to alert the flock.

Seasonal Movement: Chickadee flocks have varied movement. Some stay near their breeding territories if food is available, while other flocks drift north in spring and south in autumn.

SONG SPARROW
Melospiza melodia
L 6–7 in (15–44 cm)

Habitat: Gardens, marshes, busy countryside. The song sparrow ranges from mountains to arid regions.

Field Marks: Song sparrows have a streaked breast with a dark spot in the center. The broad eyebrow is grayish, a broad brown stripe borders the whitish throat, upper parts are brown, and underparts are white with streaks.

Behavior: The song sparrow, known for its frequent songs, is one of the most common birds in North America. During the breeding phase, the male establishes a territory of about ½ to 1½ acres (.2 to .6 hectare). When the male encounters an intruder, he ruffles his feathers and keeps his body at a horizontal angle. He lifts one or both wings, and sometimes the wings vibrate as he sings a warbling song. Another song sparrow display includes fluffed crest feathers. A "tchunk" call warns of danger. It flicks its tail and wings. When the male spots a female, he swoops down and pounces on her. If she is his mate, she will respond with a "trill" call and sit very still. Copulation follows this advance. If the female isn't his mate, she responds by giving the "zheeeee-zheeee" threat. Male and female share nest building. Mates collect grasses, leaves, and soft bark strands to build their nest in bushes, tall weeds, small trees, or on the ground. The female does its finishing touches of the nest by lining it with fine grasses and hair. A clutch of three to five eggs is laid, one each day. The female incubates the eggs, leaving the nest only for short intervals. Song sparrows are victims of cowbirds that lay eggs in the nest and leave the unsuspecting sparrow to incubate and rear their offspring. Song sparrows have two, sometimes three, broods a year. Their diet consists of insects, seeds, wild fruit, and any food found in bird feeders.

Seasonal Movement: As with many species, song sparrows differ in their migration. Some travel great distances from warm climates to northern locations in early spring and return in the fall. Males arrive before females. Birds that establish breeding territories in mild or warm climate may stay year-round.

HOUSE FINCH

Carpodacus mexicanus

L 5–5½ in (12–14 cm)

Species Note: A similar species is the linnet, *Carduelis cannabina*.

Habitat: Urban, suburban, farmlands, deserts, low vegetation, semiarid landscape.

Field Marks: Similar to the sparrow in size, the male has a red forehead and breast and a rump that's sometimes orange or yellow. The head has a brown cap, and the breast and underparts are brown streaked. The female is brown streaked. Both have yellowish brown seed-eating bills and brown legs. The tail has a squared shape.

Behavior: Found in abundance around urban areas, house finches gather eagerly at bird feeders or where they find crumbs. Finches eat insects and seeds on the ground. Originally, they ranged only on the west coast of the United States, but they were introduced to the east coast in the 1940s. House finches form flocks and feed on seeds. During courtship, males pursue females while singing a warbling song. The male displays by fluttering his wings repeatedly. The female may return the song "wheat, wheat." Nests are built of small twigs, grasses, mosses, horsehair, and string, high up in dense foliage, near water. Usually four or five eggs are laid. Young fledge two weeks after hatching. House finches have one or two broods a year. Cowbirds have been known to lay eggs in their nests so that finches brood their offspring.

Seasonal Movement: Finches range from southern Canada to southern Mexico and throughout Europe and Asia. Movement varies with climate. Those birds that nest in the far north tend to migrate south, while those residing in warmer climates stay in the general area.

EUROPEAN STARLING

Sturnus vulgaris

L 7–8½ in (17–22 cm)

Species Note: This species was introduced to North America.

Habitat: Gardens, parks, cities, farms.

Field Marks: The body is stocky, the tail short and square tipped. The bird has glossy black plumage with speckles of white and a pointed, slender bill that's yellow in summer and dark in winter.

Behavior: Starlings spend their day looking for food such as insects, worms, fruit, and seeds. They have a walk described as a waddle. In late afternoon, flocks of hundreds of birds fly directly to a roost, usually in trees in warmer weather and around city buildings during colder weather. They often roost in trees with other species, such as robins, blackbirds, cowbirds, and grackles. These birds are nuisances in cities with their noise and foul messes. Nests are built in abandoned woodpecker holes, tree cavities, or crevices in buildings. A clutch of two to nine eggs is laid in a grass-lined nest. Starlings have two or three broods each season. Vocalization is variable. Calls range from a wolf whistle and a harsh "tseeer" to bill rattles, chuckles, and warbles to mimicking a bobwhite, phoebe, flicker, killdeer, or even a crow.

Seasonal Movement: Starlings have little movement in their range. They tend to stay in the same area and continue to use the same roosts throughout the year.

HOUSE WREN
Troglodytes aedon
L 4½–5¼ in (11–14 cm)

Habitat: Wooded areas, usually deciduous trees, orchards, urban yards, and gardens.

Field Marks: The body is chunky and the plumage unstreaked, gray brown with grayish underparts. Narrow black bars are on the wings and tail. The eyebrow is a lighter color, and the sharp, slightly curved bill aids insect eating. The house wren has a cocked tail.

Behavior: House wrens are easy to locate because of their warbling song, which sounds like "tsi-tsi-tsi-tsi-oodle-oodle-oodle." The male begins to sing as a way to advertise his territory in spring. He sits high on a perch to sing, and within a territory of up to ¾ acre (.3 hectare), he places sticks and twigs in possible nesting sites. The female arrives a week or two later, and when the male recognizes her presence, his song becomes more shrill. He displays by holding wings away from the body while fluttering them. To attract her to a nest site, the male flies with heavy wing beats and lands near it. This display is repeated over and over.

The female inspects each nesting site and begins nest building if she decides to breed there. The female lines the nest of her choice and adds more twigs if needed. The nest might be in a birdhouse, a drainpipe, an abandoned woodpecker's hole, or even a coat pocket.

House wrens are notorious for nesting in strange places. Usually five or six eggs are laid. The female does all the incubating. The male comes near and sings a quiet warbling song. He will not enter the nest until after the young have hatched. The male brings food to the nest and passes it to the female, who feeds the young.

If intruders are near, the house wren holds its body horizontally and spreads its wings and lowers the tail. A series of buzz calls warn of danger. When the first brood has fledged, the male cleans the nesting site and begins his courtship behavior again. It is not unusual for him to find a new mate for the second brood. Wrens have a diet of insects, spiders, millipedes, caterpillars, and snails. They have been known to break eggs of other bird species.

Seasonal Movement: House wrens are migratory and fly to warm climates for the winter. During this time they are quiet and secretive. This species is found throughout North America and South America.

RED-WINGED
BLACKBIRD
Agelaius phoeniceus
L 8¾ in (22–23 cm)

Habitat: Marshes, dry fields, orchards, and woodlands.

Field Marks: The male has glossy black plumage with bright red shoulder patches with a buff edge. The female has brown streaked plumage with a slight red shoulder patch trimmed in yellow and a red tinge at the throat. Females are often mistaken as sparrows. (Red-winged blackbirds are slightly larger with longer bills.) The legs and bill are dark.

Behavior: Territorial and courtship behavior includes the song spread display in which the male, while perching, arches his head forward and spreads his wings to expose the bright red patches. The tail is spread and pointed downwards. An "oakalee" song accompanies this display. In song flight behavior, the male flies or glides from one perch to another and exposes his red shoulder patches. He spreads his tail and holds his head downwards. In a territorial display between two birds, the bill tilt is when both come together at their territorial boundaries and face each other. They expose red wing patches and lift bills high. After a brief moment, one bird flies away. Red-winged blackbirds defend territory of about ⅛ to ¼ acre (.05 to .1 hectare). The female constructs the nest of reeds or grasses. Often nests are suspended from several vertical branches or reeds. Three to five eggs are laid in a single brood each year. When danger approaches the nest, the female gives a "ch-ch-chee-chee" call as a warning. The male gives a harsh "check" call.

Seasonal Movement: Males migrate north to the breeding grounds in the spring a few weeks before females. In August, when the birds go through their annual molt, they seek seclusion. Just before fall migration, males reappear at the marshes and form flocks for their southward migration. Females and immature offspring migrate a few weeks later.

BLUE-GRAY TANAGER, *Trinidad*

© J. DELEVORYAS

BANANAQUIT, *Trinidad*

© J. DELEVORYAS

YELLOW WARBLER, *North America*

© J. DELEVORYAS

EASTERN MEADOWLARK, *North America*

J. SILLIMAN

Savanna Sparrow, *North America*

MIGRATION **Migration is simply movement between two distant areas. Seasonal migration is probably determined by the seasons, available food sources, and length of daylight. Weather and wind directions may also be factors.**

Migration distance varies with each bird species. Some, like the Arctic tern, fly 10,000 miles (16,000 km), while other species, like the house finch, stay in the same general area year-round.

Scientists think learning the migration route is both instinctual and learned from adults. Birds memorize the way by recognizing landscape features and possibly through sensing magnetic fields. No one knows what clues birds use to find their way through overcast skies and over great expanses of ocean. In clear weather it's thought that the sun, moon, and stars aid them in providing directions.

THORN BIRD, *South America* J. SILLIMAN

BOBOLINK,
Europe,
North America

© J. DELEVORYAS

AMERICAN
GOLDFINCH,
North America

© J. DELEVORYAS

COMMON TOADY
FLYCATCHER,
South America

© J. DELEVORYAS

WHITE-NAPPED
YUHINA,
Taiwan

© J. DELEVORYAS

YELLOW-HOODED
BLACKBIRD,
Trinidad

© J. DELEVORYAS

© J. DELEVORYAS

NORTHERN MOCKINGBIRD, *North America*

BLACK-THROATED GREEN WARBLER, *North America*

© J. DELEVORYAS

PYRRHULOXIA, *North America, South America*

HOODED ORIOLE, *North America*

TREE SPARROW, *Europe, North America, Australia*

N. ENAULT

BRAZILIAN CARDINAL, *South America*

WHITE-BROWED SCRUBWREN, *Australia*

SUPERB WREN, *Australia*

NORTHERN CARDINAL, *North America*

WILLY WAGTAIL,
Australia

WHITE-BREASTED
NUTHATCH,
North America

COMMON MYNA,
Thailand

GRAY BUTCHERBIRD,
Australia

BLUEBIRD,
North America

DARK-EYED JUNCO, *North America*

RAVEN, *North America*

HORNED LARK, *North America*

DIAMOND FIRETAIL, *Australia*

KISKADEE, *Trinidad*

GREEN BEE-EATER, *India*

AMERICAN DIPPER, *North America*

C. NEWMAN

GREENFINCH, *England, Europe*

CHAFFINCH, *Europe, Iceland, England*

BLACKBIRD, *Europe, England*

MIKE DANZENBAKER

ENGLISH ROBIN, *England, Europe*

JACKDAW, *England, Europe*

MISTLE THRUSH, *England, Europe*

ROCK DOVE (COMMON DOMESTIC PIGEON)
Columba livia
L 12½–14 in (31–36 cm)

Species Note: The rock dove was introduced worldwide from Europe.

Habitat: City parks, fields.

Field Marks: The rock dove has a plump body, broad shoulders, small head, short neck, and a short and rounded bill with slitlike nostrils. Plumage varies from light gray to lead colored with blue gray, iridescent feathers on the head and neck with a white rump and a black band on the tail. Two black bars are across each wing, head and neck are darker than the back, and it has red feet and legs.

Behavior: Commonly found in city parks, flocks of rock doves or pigeons come into close proximity with humans. They have been known to fly in excess of 84 miles (135 km) per hour. A courtship and territorial display called the bow involves the male ruffling his neck feathers while lowering the head, and turning circles or semicircles. Another display, the tail drag, may alternate with the bow behavior. The male lifts his head, spreads his tail feathers, and drags them on the ground as he runs a short distance. He makes a low cooing sound during this display. Both males and females use wing flapping in flight that makes a clapping sound. The flight pattern may include gliding with wings held high and tail feathers spread. Pairs often preen each other. Females put their bills into the males' mouth and they both will bob their heads up and down. They defend only the immediate nest area. The nest site is usually a ledge, under bridges, in barns, and in caves or similar structures. Nests are made of sticks and grasses. Usually two eggs are laid. Pigeons have two or three broods a year.

Seasonal Movement: Pigeons have no seasonal movement. They stay where food and shelter are available. All continents have a wide distribution of this species.

AMERICAN WHITE PELICAN

Pelecanus erythrorhynchos

L 62 in (157 cm) / W 108 in (274 cm)

Wt 10 to 30 lb (4.5–13.5 kg)

Habitat: Open freshwater lakes.

Field Marks: This large, heavy bird has white plumage with black wing tips. Its massive bill is 15 inches (38 cm) long and bright orange. It has a huge throat pouch and hooked bill. During breeding season a fibrous plate grows on the upper mandible which is shed after egg laying.

do brown pelicans. When taking off from water, the bird runs while flapping its wings to get its heavy body airborne. In flight, pelicans are known for aerial acrobatics. Flight is characterized by flapping, soaring, or gliding. Courtship and breeding are brief. Adult birds nest in large inland lake colonies. The American white pelican builds its nest of twigs and sticks heaped on the ground hidden by reeds, or the pelican sometimes lines a shallow, scraped-out impression in the soil with feathers. Pelicans also nest in trees. Two to three eggs are laid. Both male and female incubate eggs and offspring. In

Webbed feet are orange. Males are slightly larger than females.

Behavior: Often found in flocks, white pelicans sometimes fly in a V-formation. They fish together by forming a line or semicircle to drive fish to shallow water. They scoop up fish in a large pouch which can hold as much as 12 quarts (12 litres) of water. White pelicans fish from the surface rather than diving from the air as

feeding, the chicks put their bills inside the adult's throat to get partially digested fish. Vocalization is limited to a few gruntlike sounds; young sometimes make a screaming sound.

Seasonal Movement: White pelicans winter in southern coastal regions and then fly north and inland in spring, the breeding season.

HAIRY WOODPECKER
Picoides villosus
L 8½–10½ in (21–27 cm)

Habitat: Open or dense woodland, river groves.

Field Marks: The hairy woodpecker is larger but has almost identical markings as the downy woodpecker. Another difference is the hairy woodpecker's large bill. The back is white with wings barred with rows of white spots. The male has a red patch on the back of the head, which the female lacks. Underparts are black and white; the back is dark with white spots and a broad, white stripe. It has unmarked white outer tail feathers, short legs, and feet with strong claws for tree climbing. Two toes point forward and two point backwards to aid in this.

Behavior: Courtship begins in winter as both males and females drum on trees or other hard surfaces to attract a mate. It also is a way to claim territory. Accompanying this auditory display are swooping flights with wing fluttering made just before landing. Loud wing flapping is also part of its courtship ritual. Hairy woodpeckers make a loud "peek" call to keep track of the location of their mates. A "whinny" call is sounded during breeding and also to claim breeding territory, which is usually about ¼ acre (.1 hectare). A nest cavity is excavated from a dead or dying tree by both sexes. An average clutch is four to six eggs. Both adults take turns incubating the eggs.

Young are well developed by the time they fledge. As soon as they are able to feed themselves, the young leave the territory. Adults keep their territorial range of 6 to 8 acres (2.4 to 3.2 hectares) for life. Feeding habits include hopping around on trunks and the undersides of branches. The woodpecker uses its chisel-like bill to dig out insects and grubs from tree bark. Other food sources include berries, acorns, hazelnuts, and food from feeders, like suet, sunflower seeds, nuts, fruit, and peanut butter. When approached by a human intruder, the hairy woodpecker moves to the back of the tree trunk or flies to safety.

Seasonal Movement: Hairy woodpeckers do not migrate, but they move a short distance from their normal range in winter if food is scarce. First-year birds usually move only a few miles or kilometres from where they were hatched to establish territories. They remain in this territory for life.

BELTED KINGFISHER
Ceryle alcyon
L 13 in (33 cm)

Species Note: Many species of varying sizes are in the kingfisher family throughout the world.

Habitat: Lakes, streams, rivers, coasts; usually freshwater, but on occasion, saltwater.

Field Marks: The belted kingfisher has a stocky body and blue gray plumage on the upper body with white underbody and a gray breast band. The female has a second breast band of rust. The head is large with a ragged crest. The bill is long and the feet small.

Behavior: The belted kingfisher is solitary by nature. It defends a narrow feeding territory during the nonbreeding fall and winter. In the spring and summer, the territory is expanded and defended by both male and female. Feeding and nesting areas may not be located together. The bird gives a rattle call as a warning or in times of excitement. Head or tail bobbing accompanies this vocalization. The crest feathers also rise at this time. Kingfishers prefer a diet of fish, but they will eat tadpoles, lizards, snakes, insects, mice, crayfish, mussels, young birds, and occasionally, berries. Along the coast, kingfishers eat clams, oysters, and crabs. This bird is often seen on a perch, like a dead branch, or hovering over the water while waiting for fish to swim by. It dives, catching fish, which are killed by beating them against a branch. The fish are swallowed head first. Males establish territories for breeding range before females arrive. Courtship displays are limited. Usually the pair shares activities. Nests are built in the ground with an entrance below a cutaway bank of clay and sandy soil. The belted kingfisher excavates with the bill, and kicks the soil backwards with its feet. There is a 3- to 6-foot (1- to 2-metre) tunnel which leads to a chamber where both male and female incubate five to seven eggs. Kingfishers have one brood a year.

Seasonal Movement: Kingfishers move to a warmer climate if their breeding range freezes and fishing becomes limited. Kingfishers migrate as far south as Central America during the fall and winter. In territories where the water is open, the birds may stay year-round.

HUMMINGBIRD FAMILY
Trochilidae
L 2¾–9 in (7–23 cm)

Twenty-one species of hummingbirds are in North America, with only eight species ranging north above the Mexican border. Only four species are seen north of the Canadian border. No one species ranges over all North America, and a vast number of species are in Central America and South America. There are more than 32 species worldwide. This description applies to all hummingbird species.

Habitat: Hummingbirds are found at all altitudes and anywhere there are flowers from which to obtain nectar. They are found in all climates and migrate to escape cold weather conditions. They do not nest in aquatic or grassland habitats. Hummingbirds are frequent inhabitants of urban gardens as well as deserts, mountains, and tropical jungles.

Field Marks: Plumage is a dazzling combination of iridescent colors which vary with each species—green, red, rufus, black, blue, white, and purple. Males are generally more colorful than females and have bright colors on their gorget, or throat feathers. In poor light the iridescent feathers look black. Bills are long and needlelike for extracting nectar from flowers. Wings have large flight muscles which enable the bird to fly backwards, hover, and make rapid changes of flight path.

Behavior: Hummingbirds have the highest metabolism of any warm-blooded vertebrate in the world. They burn energy at an incredible rate and must feed continuously to survive. At night or during temporary cold weather, they fall into a lethargic state to conserve energy. In summer, males establish territories and aggressively keep other hummingbirds away from their food sources. They use displays of diving, looping, and sudden changes of direction not only for guarding territories, but also as a courtship ritual. When hovering, wings move in a figure-eight pattern.

Males are polygamous and mate with more than one female. Females establish

nesting territories and drive out all other hummingbirds, including the male. Nest building is entirely done by the female. Nests are built above the ground and are so small it is difficult to discover their location. These cup-shaped nests are made of grasses, lichens, spider webs, and soft materials. Two eggs, about the size of a pea, are laid. Hummingbirds have as many as three broods a year.

Vocalization is a squeaky call, usually made when defending a territory.

Food sources include nectar from flowers, extracted by sticking the long bill into the flower and sipping nourishment with a long protractile tongue. In the process of getting the nectar, the bird picks up pollen on its head. It rubs off this pollen on other plants as it feeds. Hum-

mingbirds are important in the pollination process of many plants. Other foods consumed are insects and spiders. Feeders attract many hummingbirds. Many aerial battles are fought for feeding rights. It isn't uncommon to see a male sitting on a high perch nearby guarding this food source.

Seasonal Movement: Hummingbirds such as the ruby-throated hummingbird fly from the summer breeding territory as far north as Canada and south to Central America. This tiny bird can cross 4,500 to 5,000 miles (7,200 to 8,000 km) over the Gulf of Mexico in one continuous flight. Other species migrate south to avoid cold weather. An exception is the Anna's hummingbird that stays in its mild weather range year-round.

CHESTNUT MANDIBLED TOUCAN, *South America*

RESPLENDENT QUETZAL, *South America*

BLUE-CROWNED
MOTMOT, *Trinidad*

© J. DELEVORYAS

RED-AND-GREEN
MACAW, *South America*

COLLARED TROGON, *South America*

© J. DELEVORYAS

MOURNING DOVE, *North America*

SPOTTED TURTLEDOVE, *Australia*

COCKATIEL, *Australia*

RAINBOW LORIKEETS, *Australia*

MAJOR MITCHELL'S COCKATOO,
Australia

BLEEDING-HEART DOVE, *Philippines*

SULPHUR-CRESTED COCKATOO,
Australia

SACRED KINGFISHER, *Australia*

BAND-TAILED PIGEON, *North America*

KOOKABURRA, *Australia*

LAUGHING KOOKABURRA   **Aborigine folklore tells how the kookaburra, with its noisy song, called up the sun from its bed each morning, and that if humans joined the bird in chorus, that would delay awakening the day. Early settlers in Australia thought the bird's raucous call was that of woodland spirits.**

Known as the Bushman's clock, these husky birds begin to sing at daybreak in the hope of attracting mates or warning other birds that the territory is taken. The kookaburra repeats its songs at dusk. It's been said that the kookaburra calls in the early morning when light is poor for hunting, and later in the day, it sits quietly high in a tree to wait for prey, like lizards, snakes, small rodents, or insects, to crawl into view on the ground below. With a precision attack, this patient hunter swoops down and plucks up prey with its large, strong beak.

The kookaburra makes its home in wooded areas. Although it belongs to the kingfisher family, it isn't an aquatic hunter like other species. This short-legged bird is stocky and has a large head with a 3-inch (7.5-cm) bill. Feathers are reddish brown, black, white, and gray with a blue gray patch on the wings. Adults grow to 16–18 inches (40–45 cm) long and weigh slightly less than a pound (.45 kg).

It lays two to four eggs in a nest high in the trees. Adults that do not mate help defend the birds' territory and feed the young. Kookaburras are nonmigratory.

MAGELLANTIC PENGUINS, *South America*

FAIRY PENGUINS, *Australia*

MALE & FEMALE OSTRICH, *Africa*

OSTRICH (*Struthio camelus*) **Millions of years ago nine species of ostrich existed. Today, only one species survives, in eastern Africa and in southern Australia, where they were introduced.**

As the largest living bird, the ostrich grows to about 8 feet (240 cm) and weighs around 300 pounds (135 kg). These flightless birds are well adapted for living in open, arid environments where predators are common. Their long necks give them a good view over great land expanses. The eye, about the size of a tennis ball, measures about 2 inches (5 cm) across. Their keen eyesight allows them to detect distant disturbances and makes them wary.

The plumage is different for the sexes. Males can be identified by their black plumes with white on the wings and tail. Females are brown with pale edging on the feathers. The head, neck, and legs of both genders are almost naked. The eyes have long black eyelashes. Feet have two toes with a long claw on the largest toe.

Ostriches inhabit dry areas and are constantly searching for food. Their diet consists of seeds, leaves, fruits, and small animals such as insects, lizards, and small tortoises. When water isn't available, they get needed fluids by eating succulent plants.

These huge birds have been seen travelling in large herds led by either a dominant cock (male) or hen (female). When breeding takes place, a male collects a harem of three to five hens. This may happen any time of year. At this time, the male develops a red pigment on his head and begins to display. Each male establishes his own territory. The male then launches into an elaborate courtship ritual, which consists of synchronizing the head and neck movements with the hen and making great flourishes of wing plumes. At the climax of these displays, mating occurs.

Hens usually lay six to eight eggs in a communal nest that's simply a shallow, scooped-out depression in the ground. This nest can measure almost 3 feet (1 m) across. Egg-laying may take a period of 20 days. These eggs weigh 2½ pounds (over a kilogram) and measure 6 inches (15 cm) long. Shells are thick and strong.

The dominant hen drives other members of the harem away, leaving herself and the cock to incubate the eggs. The male incubates the eggs at night, and the female takes over during the day. Rather than keeping the eggs warm, the massive bodies of the adults shade the eggs. Hatching occurs after 39 to 42 days. It takes more than a day for the chick to break out of the thick eggshell. The chick's stiff plumage is brown and speckled.

Chicks can run immediately and within a month they'll be able to run at almost 35 miles an hour. Young ostriches are vulnerable to predators, especially jackals. Adult ostriches lead their chicks away from harm, and if threatened, they perform displays to distract predators, while chicks run and crouch for safety.

When chicks are able, they form large groups or bands for safety. At 4 or 5 years old, they begin to breed.

Predators respect the lethal kick of an adult ostrich. Rather than fight, however, an ostrich usually flees with strides of 10 feet (over 3 m) at a speed of 35 to 40 miles (64 km) an hour.

RUFOUS HUMMINGBIRD,
North America,
South America

GILA WOODPECKER,
North America

NORTHERN FLICKER, *North America*

GROUND HORNBILL, *Africa*

HOOPOE, *India, Africa*

Birding Organizations

Australia
Royal Australian Ornithologists' Union
21 Gladstone Street
Moonee Ponds, Victoria 3039
Australia

Bird Observers Club of Australia
P.O. Box 185
Nunawading, Victoria 3131
Australia

Canada
Federation of Alberta Naturalists
P.O. Box 1472
Edmonton, Alberta
Canada T5J 2N5

Federation of British Columbia Naturalists
1200 Hornby Street
Vancouver, British Columbia
Canada V6Z 2E6

Manitoba Naturalists Society
302-128 James Avenue
Winnipeg, Manitoba
Canada V8W 2Z2

New Brunswick Federation of Naturalists
% New Brunswick Museum
277 Douglas Avenue
Saint John, New Brunswick
Canada E2K 1E5

Newfoundland Natural History Society
P.O. Box 1013
Saint John's, Newfoundland
Canada A1C 5M3

Nova Scotia Bird Society
Nova Scotia Museum
1747 Summer Street
Halifax, Nova Scotia
Canada B3H 3A6

Federation of Ontario Naturalists
355 Lesmill Road
London, Ontario
Canada N6E 1Z7

The Province of Quebec
Society for the Protection of Birds, Inc.
4832 de Maisonneuve Blvd. W.
Montreal, Quebec
Canada H3Z 1M5

Saskatchewan Natural History Society
P.O. Box 414
Raymore, Saskatchewan
Canada S0A 3J0

England
Royal Society for the Protection of Birds
The Lodge
Sandy, Bedfordshire
SG19 2DL England

New Zealand
Ornithological Society of New Zealand
% P.O. Box 12397
Wellington, New Zealand

United States
National Audubon Society
950 Third Avenue
New York, New York 10022
U.S.A.

American Birding Association
P.O. Box 4335
Austin, Texas 78765
U.S.A.

National Wildlife Federation
1412 Sixteenth Street N.W.
Washington, D.C. 20036
U.S.A.

Index